JAPAN
the land

Bobbie Kalman

A Bobbie Kalman Book

The Lands, Peoples, and Cultures Series

 Crabtree Publishing Company

www.crabtreebooks.com

The Lands, Peoples, and Cultures Series
Created by Bobbie Kalman

For Marc

Written by
Bobbie Kalman

Coordinating editor
Ellen Rodger

Editor
Jane Lewis

Contributing editor
Lisa Gurusinghe

Production coordinator
Rose Gowsell

Production
Arlene Arch

Editors/first edition
Janine Schaub
Christine Arthurs
Margaret Hoogeveen
Christine McClymont

Separations and film
Embassy Graphics

Printer
Worzalla Publishing Company

Photographs
Carol Baum: p. 9 (top); Joan Mann, Cameramann Int'l., Ltd.: p. 3, 20 (both), 21 (both), 23 (bottom), 25, 26; Robert Holmes: p. 31 (bottom); courtesy of Japan Information Centre: p. 8 (bottom right); courtesy of Japan National Tourist Organization: p. 8 (bottom left), 9 (bottom), 12, 18, 19, 22, 29; Margus Jukkum: p. 9 (bottom); Gayle McDougall: p. 15; AFP/Corbis: p. 24; Royal Ontario Museum: p. 14; Robert Sischy: p. 16 (top), 30 (top); Tom Skudra: p. 30 (bottom right); Tony Stone/Masterfile: p. 8 (top); Elias Wakan/Pacific Rim Slide Bank: p. 16 (bottom), 17; Michael S. Yamashita/Corbis: p. 10, 11, 23 (top), 27, 31 (top); other images by Digital Stock

Map
Jim Chernishenko

Illustrations
Dianne Eastman: icons
David Wysotski, Allure Illustrations: back cover

Cover: Japanese gardens are favorite places to relax.

Title page: Many Japanese people enjoy spending time in nature, enjoying the natural beauty of their country.

Icon: Cherry blossoms

Back cover: Red-faced Japanese snow monkeys earned their name by surviving in areas with harsh winters.

Published by
Crabtree Publishing Company

PMB 16A
350 Fifth Avenue
Suite 3308
New York
N.Y. 10118

612 Welland Avenue
St. Catharines
Ontario, Canada
L2M 5V6

73 Lime Walk
Headington
Oxford OX3 7AD
United Kingdom

Cataloging in Publication Data

Kalman, Bobbie, 1947
  Japan, the land / Bobbie Kalman. – Rev. ed.
  p.cm – (The lands, peoples, and cultures series)
  Includes index.
  ISBN 0-7787-9375-3 (RLB) -- ISBN 0-7787-9743-0 (pbk.)
  1. Japan–Juvenile literature. [1. Japan.] I. Title. II Series.
  DS806 .K33 2001
  952–dc21   00-057084
                                                         LC

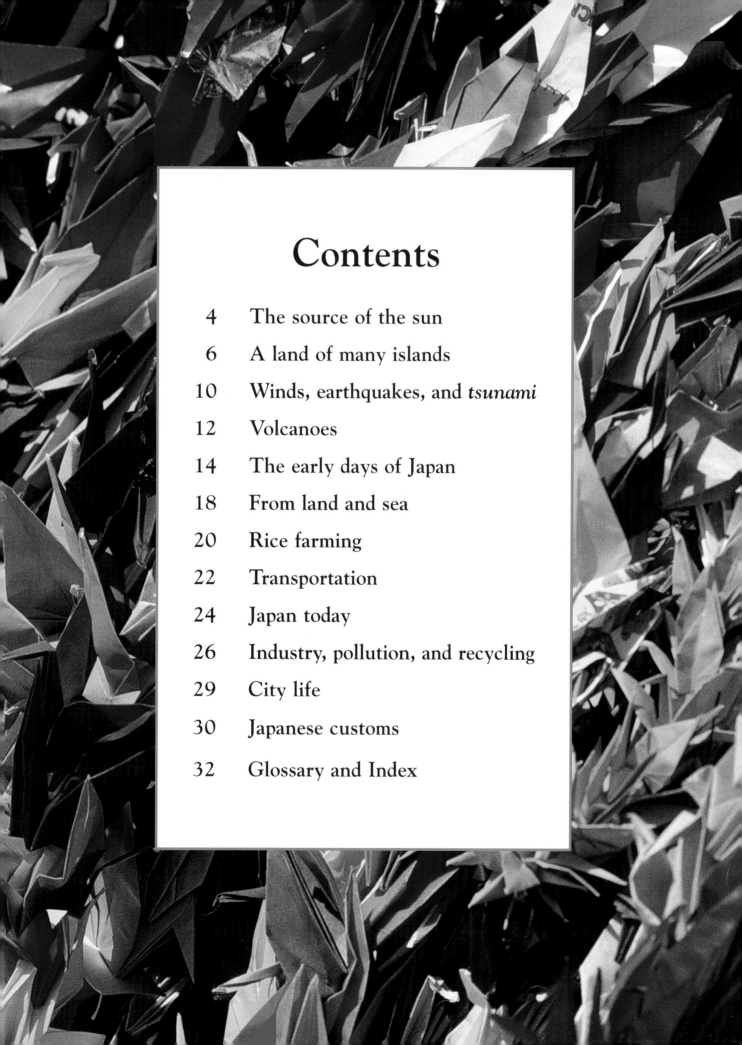

Contents

The source of the sun

Thousands of years ago, the Chinese saw the sun rise over the islands to the east and they named this country *jih-pen*. *Jih-pen* means "the source of the sun." This land came to be known as Japan by the English-speaking world. Japanese people call their country *Nippon*. The sun is an important symbol in Japan. It is represented by the red circle on the Japanese national flag.

Nature is an important part of Japanese **culture**. Although most of Japan's 126 million citizens live in crowded cities, they make regular outings to enjoy the lush beauty of the countryside. Each year, millions of Japanese people travel around their island nation to experience and appreciate the bamboo forests, majestic mountains, fast-flowing rivers, and picturesque coastlines.

A land of many islands

Japan is made up of about one thousand small islands and four large ones: Honshu, Shikoku, Kyushu, and Hokkaido. Most of the population lives on Honshu, which is the largest island. Japan is only 249 miles (400 km) wide at its widest point, so no matter where you go, the seashore is never far away.

Mountainous interiors

Mountains cover almost three quarters of Japan's land area. The bases of the mountains along the coast provide the only flat land in the country. Cities, industries, and farms must share this small area. Almost half of the country's huge population is crowded onto a thin strip of land that is less than three percent of Japan's total area.

Fujisan

The island of Honshu contains Japan's highest mountains, including the Japanese Alps and Mount Fuji. Fuji is the highest mountain in Japan, standing at 12,388 feet (3776 m) high. This majestic mountain, which Japanese people call *Fujisan*, is about sixty-two miles (100 km) from Tokyo. Each year, thousands of people climb to the top of Mount Fuji.

(opposite page, top) Many Japanese people climb Mount Fuji at least once in their lifetime. It takes between five and nine hours to reach the top.

(below) Japan's closest neighbors are China, Korea, and Russia.

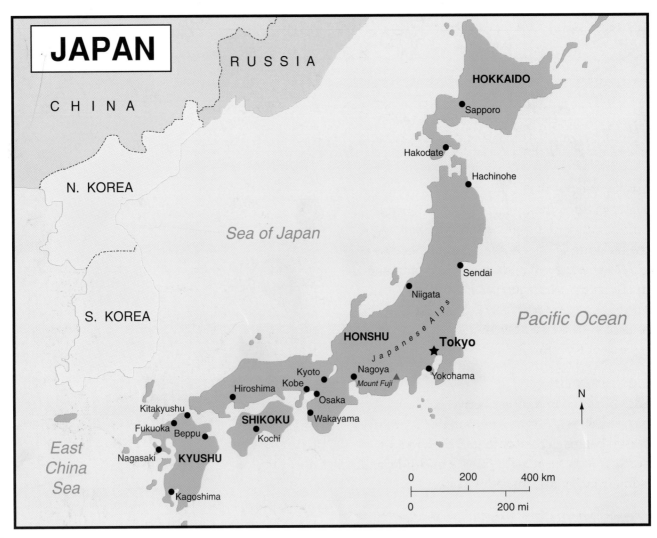

Early blossoms

The **climate** of the central region of Japan is mild for most of the year, but temperatures in the far north and south vary greatly. In January, village streets on the island of Hokkaido and in the northwestern part of Honshu are often buried under several feet of snow. At the same time of year, flowers bloom in the southern regions of Kyushu.

Lots of rain

Each year, Japan receives between 39 and 118 inches (100 and 300 cm) of rainfall. The rainy season begins in the south and then moves north. It lasts from early June to mid-July, and is followed by hot, humid weather.

Japan's countryside is lush and picturesque.

Although the climate of Japan is mild, the northern regions receive plenty of snow.

Almost three quarters of Japan's people live in busy, congested cities. The most crowded of all is Tokyo.

(opposite, top) Japanese farms produce three quarters of the nation's food by using modern machines and efficient farming methods.

(right) Even the most natural-looking gardens in Japan have been carefully planned to capture the fragile beauty of nature.

(below) Some of Japan's many islands are just rocks that stick up above the water line.

 # Winds, earthquakes, and *tsunami*

Japan is located on an unstable area of the earth's surface. The **earth's crust** is not one smooth layer like an eggshell. It is made up of several big pieces called plates. These plates move and shift very slowly. Some are moving towards one another, and others are moving apart. Japan is located near the edge of a plate. The movement of this plate causes earthquakes, volcanoes, and giant waves.

A dangerous dragon

An old legend describes the islands of Japan as the back of a huge, sleeping sea dragon. Whenever the dragon stirs in its sleep, it causes an earthquake. The most devastating earthquake in Japan's history happened on September 1, 1923.

It left the cities of Tokyo and Yokohama in ruins and resulted in over 100,000 deaths. The quake struck at noon, just as people were lighting fires on which they would prepare their lunches. Most of the damage was caused by these fires, which spread quickly throughout the cities. Japan's next big earthquake occurred in Kobe in 1995. More than five thousand people died and over 100,000 homes were destroyed. A major city highway, which was built to withstand an earthquake, collapsed.

(above) A young man walks his bike through an earthquake damaged area in Kobe, Japan.

(opposite) Bathing in hot-spring baths is relaxing.

10

Earthquake drills

Although nothing can be done to prevent an earthquake, people can prepare for one. Japanese buildings are constructed to absorb the shock of large **tremors**. Office workers and school children have regular earthquake drills. During these drills, people turn off their gas stoves and electric heaters to prevent fires. They then find shelter under a table or in a doorway. Many homes have earthquake survival kits containing food and medicine.

Giant waves

Earthquakes can happen on land or at sea. When an earthquake occurs under the sea, it often creates a *tsunami*. A *tsunami* is a massive wave that can be as tall as a giant ferris wheel! A *tsunami* hits the shoreline like a huge wall of water, causing floods and destroying buildings. In 1703, one *tsunami* killed over 100,000 people in the city of Awa. At one time, *tsunami* were mistakenly called tidal waves, but they have no connection with tides.

Hot springs

The movement of the earth's plates that causes earthquakes also creates hot springs. Hot springs, called *onsen*, are natural pools filled with water heated deep inside the earth. *Onsen* are a source of great pleasure and entertainment. One of the most popular bathing spots in Japan is a hot-spring spa in the small city of Beppu. Millions of people visit Beppu each year to relax in its steamy pools and admire the forest scenery.

Typhoons

At the end of summer, huge storms form that resemble hurricanes. These storms are called typhoons. Typhoon is a Chinese word meaning "great wind." Typhoons are so strong that they can blow down trees and topple buildings. They often cause floods and landslides in the coastal areas. When a typhoon warning is announced over the radio, everyone goes home immediately. The streets empty, and traffic stops. It is important to be in a protected place indoors when a typhoon strikes.

 # Volcanoes

Japan's mountains were formed by volcanoes. When the earth's plates move, melted rock, called magma, is forced up from inside the earth through cracks or long, narrow passages in the Earth's crust. When magma comes in contact with air, it becomes lava. Lava burns everything in its path. The lava cools and hardens into rock.

After a volcano has erupted hundreds of times, the layers of hardened lava eventually build up to form a mountain.

(above) Some active volcanoes constantly spew out smoke and gases.

(opposite) Mount Fuji is a dormant volcano.

Active volcanoes

Volcanoes that erupt from time to time are called active volcanoes. An active volcano can mean disaster for nearby communities. Along with burning lava, an eruption also creates clouds of black smoke, gases, and sometimes enough ash to bury entire buildings. The people who live close to active volcanoes must be ready to flee at a moment's notice! Ten percent of the world's active volcanoes—sixty-seven in all—are found in Japan.

Volcanoes that do not erupt

Most of Japan's volcanoes are not active. Volcanoes that have not erupted for hundreds of years, but still might erupt, are called dormant volcanoes. Mount Fuji, the most famous of Japan's 200 volcanoes, is a dormant volcano. Its last eruption was in 1707. A volcano that has not erupted for thousands of years is called extinct.

Volcano facts

- When a volcano is about to erupt, the earth trembles. These small rumblings are caused by magma squeezing through cracks inside the ground.

- Lava can flow as fast as a river or creep along at a snail's pace.

- A volcano sometimes lets off gases that smell like rotten eggs!

- A volcano can spew a fiery fountain into the sky that is as high as the CN Tower in Toronto, Canada. This tower is the world's tallest free-standing structure and is over 1800 feet (550 m) tall.

- Clouds of smoke, steam, and ash from a large volcano cause beautiful sunsets.

The early days of Japan

The Ainu

The first group of people to live in Japan were the Ainu. These native people look slightly different from other Japanese people. They have more body hair and paler skin. About 2500 Ainu still live in Japan, but fewer than 200 are of full Ainu **ancestry**. These **indigenous people** now live in the northern part of Japan on the island of Hokkaido.

Asian influences

Most Japanese people are not **descendants** of the Ainu. Most Japanese citizens descended from Chinese and Korean people who came to Japan long ago. These people brought their own languages, government, religion, and skills with them to Japan. Modern Japanese culture emerged as a result of these cultures.

Clans and emperors

Japan's **civilization** is thousands of years old. In the early days, **clans** ruled sections of the country. Clans were large, powerful families that fought against one another for land and power. In the fourth century, the leader of the Yamato clan became emperor. He claimed to be a descendant of Jinmu Tenno, who was believed to have descended from the sun goddess, Amaterasu. *Tenno,* which means "heavenly king," became the emperor's title. All Japanese emperors can trace their family line back to Jinmu Tenno.

The emperor's general

Emperors have reigned over Japan for over 1300 years. The emperor was not always the most powerful person in the land, however. The real power often belonged to military clans. In 1192, a man named Minamoto Yoritomo took control and ruled over all the clans. He was called *shogun. Shogun* means the "emperor's general." This powerful man made all the laws on behalf of the emperor.

Feuding feudal lords

Daimyo were **feudal** lords. Each *daimyo* controlled an area of Japan, and the *shogun* ruled over the *daimyo*. The *samurai*, meaning "ones who serve," were the soldiers of the *daimyo*. The *daimyo* and their *samurai* often tried to win more land and power by fighting against other *daimyo*. For protection, the castle of a *daimyo* was surrounded by a moat and located on high ground.

Japanese knights

The *samurai* were similar to the knights of **medieval** Europe. A *samurai's* armor was made of metal plates held together by colorful cords. His weapons were the bow and arrow, a curved dagger, and a long steel sword. The *samurai* lived by "The Code of the Warriors," called *bushido. Bushido* instructed them in religion and **martial arts** and taught them about loyalty, self-control, and noble behavior. The *samurai* believed that loyalty to their lord was the most important quality that a soldier could possess.

(left) A sculpture of Minamoto Yoritomo, Japan's first shogun.

(opposite page) A samurai statue guards the entrance to an old shogun palace. A sword, dagger, and bow and arrows were traditional samurai weapons.

A privileged class

At one time, the *samurai* were the only people who rode horses, carried swords, and used last names. All these things were restricted to those who were thought to be of noble birth. Only a small portion of the population of Japan belonged to the privileged *samurai* class. The rest of society was made up of farmers, **artisans**, merchants, priests, and monks. Although the *samurai* had many privileges, the merchants and artisans were often much wealthier.

Sealed off from the world

For 700 years, Japan was ruled by *shogun* and their *samurai*. About 300 years ago, the *shogun* made a law called the Isolation Decree. This law prevented Japanese people from having contact with the outside world. No one was allowed to travel outside Japan, and no foreigners were permitted to enter the country. The people in positions of power believed that the way to have a unified country was to make sure that only Japanese ways were learned.

New ideas

In 1853, an American military officer named Commodore Perry arrived on Japan's shores with a fleet of steamships. He demanded that the *shogun* allow Americans to trade with Japan. The Japanese were not strong enough to fight the **invaders** and were forced to open their ports to the outside world. This event marked the beginning of a number of major changes. Many new ideas flooded into the country. Japanese people soon learned about railways, factories, steam power, electricity, and hundreds of other inventions.

Fifteen years later, the ruling *shogun* was forced to resign, and Emperor Meiji gained power. Less than one hundred years later, after World War II, Japan became a **democracy**. Today, Japan is governed by a group of elected representatives called the Diet. The head of the government is the prime minister. Japan still has an emperor, who is an important and respected figure, but he does not make political decisions.

Test your *samurai* knowledge

How much do you know about *samurai* life? If you don't know the answers to these questions, how well can you guess? Write your answers down on a piece of paper.

1. The word *samurai* means:
   a) one who fights
   b) one who serves
   c) one who rides a horse

2. A favorite *samurai* game was:
   a) *go*
   b) Chinese checkers
   c) marbles

3. At the age of seven a *samurai* boy received:
   a) wide trousers
   b) a sword
   c) a birthday cake

4. At the age of fifteen a *samurai* boy received:
   a) a sword
   b) a haircut
   c) both *a* and *b*

5. Before going to war, *samurai* warriors ate three lucky foods. These were:
   a) rice, fish, **miso** soup
   b) mashed potatoes, pickles, jellybeans
   c) shellfish, seaweed, chestnuts

6. The *samurai* hairstyle was:
   a) short spikes
   b) bald in front, ponytail in back
   c) bald all over

7. Before battle, a *samurai* warrior sometimes:
   a) brushed his teeth
   b) blackened his teeth
   c) made a will

8. After battle, a *samurai* warrior enjoyed:
   a) sumo wrestling
   b) a nap
   c) the tea **ceremony**

9. *Samurai* armor was difficult to wear because:
   a) the cords tying the metal plates together got heavy when it rained
   b) the cords froze when it snowed
   c) the cords were often full of lice and ants
   d) all of the above

10. *Samurai* compared themselves to:
    a) cherry blossoms
    b) horses
    c) the sun

(opposite page, top) Adult samurai *shaved only the front part of their heads;* samurai *boys shaved their heads all over, except for bangs and a topknot.*

(above and opposite page, bottom) Samurai *wore elaborate costumes and rode horses. Sometimes* samurai *women fought alongside their husbands.*

Answers: 1. b; 2. a. *Go* is a game of strategy in which one player captures another's pieces; 3. a. *Hakama* are wide trousers that were worn by the *samurai*; 4. c; 5. c; 6. b; 7. b; 8. c. The tea ceremony, a slow, **ritualistic** way of drinking tea, relaxed the *samurai* after battle; 9. d; 10. a. The *samurai* felt that their lives were as fragile and short as those of cherry blossoms.

From land and sea

Not all of Japan is crowded. Small farming communities lie nestled in lush mountain valleys. Quiet fishing villages are scattered throughout the smaller islands. Although only a small number of Japanese people live in these areas, they provide the rest of the country with most of its food supply.

A big job for a few farmers

Until the 1900s, more than half of all Japanese people farmed for a living. Now only eight percent grow food and livestock to feed the rest of the population. Many children are deciding not to stay on their parents' farms. They choose to work and live in cities. Many farmers work at other jobs in nearby cities and spend only part of the day working on the land. Machinery has made some farm work quicker. Family members help with most of the field work. Today, women and elders work on part-time farms.

Efficient farms

Japan's farms are small compared to those in other countries. The average-sized North American farm is more than 100 times larger than the average Japanese farm. Japan produces three quarters of its own food because it uses efficient farming methods. Every available space is used. It is not unusual to find crops planted on tiny plots in the middle of a city.

Terraces

Japan is famous for its terraced farmland that looks like wide stairs carved into mountainsides. Terraces enable farmers to use every bit of available land. **Erosion** is a big problem on terraced fields. These fields must be fertilized regularly to replace nutrients that get washed away by storms and flooding.

(below) Terraces enable farmers to use land on mountain slopes to grow a variety of foods.

Changing crops

The diets of Japanese people have changed drastically over the past century. For many years, peasants grew rice for their *daimyo* but could not afford to eat rice themselves. They ate only pickled vegetables, soya, and grains such as barley and millet. When **feudalism** ended, everyone could afford rice, so it became the most important crop. In recent years, however, mixed farming has taken up as much land as rice farming. One third of Japan's land is used for growing rice; another third is used for tea, wheat, fruit, and vegetables; the remaining third is reserved for raising farm animals such as cattle, pigs, and chickens.

Fishing

Fishing is a major industry in Japan. Japan catches and eats more fish than any other nation. On average, Japanese citizens eat about 100 pounds (45 kg) of fish a year. By comparison, a person living in Europe or North America eats only eleven pounds (5 kg) of fish per year. The three common kinds of fishing in Japan are: coastal fishing, fish farming, and deep-sea **trawling**. Coastal fishing includes many fishing fleets as well as independent fishermen who harvest the coastal waters for octopuses and fish such as sardines and tuna.

Fish farming

Aquaculture is a kind of "fish farming" that involves the breeding of fish in shallow waters along the coast. Yellow-tailed fish, shrimp, tuna, and oysters are examples of sea creatures that are farmed in this way. Fish-farming operations are often run by families.

Far out at sea

Some people work for large companies aboard huge fishing vessels. They live on the ships and go on fishing voyages that last up to five months. These ships are like factories because they have the equipment to preserve and freeze their catch right on board. They provide fish for both Japanese and foreign markets.

The fishing boats in the harbor are colorfully decorated for one of Japan's many festivals.

Rice farming

Hundreds of years ago, the Japanese learned rice-growing techniques from the Chinese. Rice is a staple food for Japanese people. People also use rice straw to make sandals, hats, *tatami* mats, and a type of wine called *sake*. The rice plant was originally believed to be a gift from the gods. For this reason, great ropes woven from rice straw are hung in Shinto shrines.

(this page) In the old days, seedlings were planted by hand. Today, machines do the work.

(opposite, left) Fully grown rice plants are cut down by a harvesting machine.

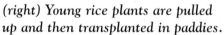

(right) Young rice plants are pulled up and then transplanted in paddies.

Two crops a year

Rice grows well in Japan's climate. Heavy rainfall, mild temperatures, and long hours of daylight allow farmers in many areas to grow two crops of rice each year. As a result, Japan produces more rice than any other Asian rice-growing country.

Planting and watering

Growing rice is a difficult process. Farmers used to do all the work by hand, but now almost everything is done by machine. At the beginning of the growing season, farmers plant rice seeds in small plots of dry land. While the seeds are sprouting, they prepare wet fields, or **paddies**, which will be used later. Rice needs plenty of water to grow. Through a system of pipes, the paddies are flooded with water from nearby rivers. Dikes, or low walls of earth, are built around sections of each paddy. They prevent the water from draining away.

Transplanting

After three or four weeks, the seeds in the dry fields grow into small plants about eight inches (20 cm) high. Then they are ready to be transplanted into the wet paddies. Transplanting and tending rice plants was a tedious and difficult job when it was done by hand. Farm workers tucked up their pant legs and waded barefoot in the paddies. Today, most transplanting is done by machine.

Harvest time

When the stalks of the plants are golden yellow, the rice is ready to be harvested. Farmers open the dikes and drain the water from the paddies. After the fields have dried, the rice is cut down by harvesting machines. In some areas, the harvest season is very wet, so the rice plants cannot be left on the ground to dry. Instead, the farmers hang the plants from elevated frames. Each village or region has its own way of bundling and hanging the rice to dry.

Threshing

Rice grains must be removed from the plant by hitting or striking it. This process, called threshing, is done by hand or machine. After threshing, the rice grains are put in sacks and transported to factories where the shell around each grain is removed. The rice is then packaged and shipped to stores.

Transportation

In the past, getting from place to place in Japan was difficult. Steep mountains made journeys dangerous and time-consuming. Traveling by river was next to impossible because most of Japan's rivers are short, rocky rapids that tumble down mountain sides.

Tunnels and bridges

Today, long tunnels through mountains and huge bridges over river valleys make traveling easier. Japan has also built watertight tunnels beneath the sea. Undersea tunnels connect the islands of Honshu, Kyushu, and Hokkaido. The tunnel to Hokkaido is almost thirty-four miles (54 km) long, making it the longest underwater tunnel in the world. Both cars and trains travel through tunnels and over bridges among the islands. Some trains run along elevated tracks above streets and others run underground in subways.

Public transportation

Although many Japanese people own cars, there is little space for parking. Most people use public transportation during the week and drive their cars only on weekends. Japan has one of the most sophisticated public transportation systems in the world.

Thousands of people spend up to four hours a day going to and from work on **commuter trains**. The train is such a popular mode of transportation that it is usually crowded, and many passengers must stand during the entire trip. Some subway stations in Tokyo employ professional "pushers" to cram people into the train during rush hours. It is necessary to shove passengers aboard to fit everyone in and allow the doors to close. The train does not start until all the doors are shut.

As fast as a speeding bullet!

The quickest and most reliable way to travel in Japan is on the *shinkansen*, or bullet trains. These trains travel as fast as 168 miles (270 km) per hour. Passengers wait near lines marked on the platform that indicate exactly where the doors of the train will open.

Faster still!

In the near future Japan hopes to be whisking train passengers along at speeds of over 300 miles (500 km) per hour. Japanese engineers are testing a new type of train known as maglev, which is short for "magnetically levitated." The maglev hovers on magnets about 4 inches (10 cm) above its track. In 1997, the maglev test line set the train at 329 miles per hour (529 km) per hour. These trains are not only fast, but extremely quiet. The only sound a bystander hears is a whoosh of air as the train speeds past.

(left) The bridge to Shikoku, Seto Ohashi, is the last link joining Japan's four main islands.

How does it work?

The maglev is on a walled track. The train and the track are fitted with metal coils. An electric current is passed through the coils to give them a magnetic charge. The charge on the track and the train can be adjusted to attract or repel each other. Controlled by a computer, this system of **electromagnets** keeps the train moving straight and at the right height above the track.

(above) The maglev is a train without wheels that looks like a cross between a shinkansen *and a spacecraft.*

(right) Even though Japan has an efficient public transit system, subway platforms become extremely crowded during rush hours.

For centuries, the majority of Japanese people were rice farmers. Cultivating rice in the old days was back-breaking work. Peasants toiled long hours to plant and tend the rice crops. This tradition of hard work has been passed on to modern industrial Japanese people. Today, Japan produces a multitude of manufactured goods. More products in electronics, computers, cars, steel, industrial machinery, and plastics are made in Japan than in any other country.

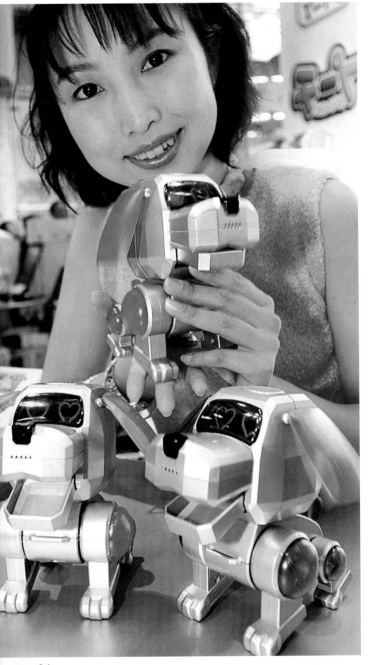

Automobiles

During the 1980s, Japan led the world in the production of automobiles. In the 1990s, however, the industry was less profitable. Other countries bought fewer Japanese cars and produced more vehicles at their own automobile plants. Today, Japan is working on creating cars that use less fuel and release fewer harmful gases, such as carbon dioxide.

Shipbuilding

Japan is an island nation, so it is not surprising that shipbuilding is one of its major industries. Oil rigs, supertankers, ferryboats, and ships with energy-saving, computer-controlled sails are just a few examples of ocean-going vessels that are manufactured in Japan.

Amazing the world with robots

Japan has been responsible for some of the world's most advanced robots. Robots in Japan have been programmed to perform thousands of jobs. Japan has seeing-eye robots to aid the blind, and robots that wait on customers in restaurants. Industrial robots are used on factory assembly lines. Robots help increase production. They perform tasks without tiring and carry out dangerous jobs such as handling **toxic** chemicals.

The Little Giant

Japan is often called the "Little Giant" because, although it is small, it is a powerful country. Japan became industrialized in half the time it took other nations to do so. Japanese people have improved their standard of living through determination, hard work, and cooperation.

(left) Pet robotic-dogs are one of the many electronic gadgets made in Japan.

(opposite) These two men are operating a robot machine designed to work on engines.

Industry, pollution, and recycling

Japan's rapid industrial growth has created a lot of pollution. Between 1950 and 1970, Japan did not put much thought or effort into pollution control. In every big city, factories spewed chemicals into the air and dumped toxic waste into the water.

Soon people in contaminated areas began to suffer from pollution-related illnesses. Many of these illnesses are now known around the world by Japanese names because they were first identified in Japan. For instance, metals such as **mercury** and **cadmium** found their way into the food chain. The disease caused by mercury poisoning is known as *minimata*, and cadmium

causes the disease *itai-itai*. *Itai-itai* means "it hurts, it hurts" in Japanese. People with these diseases suffer severe pain, brain disorders, brittle bones, and birth defects.

Pollution controls

In the 1980s and 1990s, people became more concerned about the environment, and they looked for solutions to industrial-waste problems. The Japanese government passed laws to control the huge amounts of toxic waste that industries were dumping into the air, water, and land. Industries were required to develop pollution-control devices that filtered out many of the harmful substances they produced.

(above) Workers put household goods into trucks that are going to the garbage dump.

(left) Industries continue to pollute the air and water around them. Smog is a major problem in Japan's large cities.

Seeking better solutions

These controls have helped but not solved Japan's pollution problems. Regulations and devices help prevent some pollution from entering the environment, but they do nothing about pollution that already exists. Pollution that is taken out of the air, for example, still remains as polluted dust on the land. Scientists and engineers from many countries are working toward reducing the dangers of industrial waste.

Recycling champions

In Japan, people sort all their garbage. Glass, tin, and paper are recycled and turned into useful products. The rest is taken to dumps where it is inspected for dangerous substances and then burned in large incinerators. The ash from the incinerated trash is checked to make sure it can be dumped safely into landfill sites.

Throwaway society

Every day, people throw millions of items into the garbage that are not recycled. Consumer products are often packaged in numerous layers of paper, plastic, and cardboard. Many restaurants in Japan use disposable wooden chopsticks instead of washing reusable ones. Most Japanese people do not buy secondhand appliances, bicycles, or cars. They prefer to buy the newest models, so garbage dumps are filled with these items.

City life

Most of Japan's major cities are crowded along the coast of Honshu island. Japan's biggest cities are Tokyo, Osaka, Yokohama, and Nagoya.

Tokyo, the huge capital

Twelve million people live in Tokyo, Japan's capital city. This city is one of the most densely populated areas of the world. It is made up of twenty-six smaller cities as well as fifteen towns and villages. Visitors and residents of Tokyo enjoy a wide variety of shops, restaurants, and entertainment. They can visit the *Ginza*, a famous shopping district, or *Akihabara*, where shops have the latest Japanese electronic products on display. Picnickers can find a perfect place for an afternoon picnic at the Imperial Palace gardens. In Tokyo, people can also hear music played by international rock groups, watch a traditional *kabuki* play, or spend a day at Disneyland.

Kyoto, heart of Japan

The city of Kyoto is a popular destination for Japanese travelers. Each year, fifty million people from all over the country go to Kyoto to see peaceful images of ancient Japan: women in fancy kimonos, tea houses in secluded gardens,

and tall **pagodas** outlined against the sky. Even though more than one million people live in Kyoto, it is still possible to find the wooden houses and narrow lanes of the past, just behind the busy modern streets. Two thousand temples and shrines are nestled in the tree-covered mountains that surround the city.

Coping with crowds

Almost three quarters of Japan's population live in congested cities. How do people cope with being in such small spaces with so many other people? The answer is good manners. In crowded areas such as subway stations, people do not push and shove, but patiently wait their turn. Japanese people also make the best of cramped office and living space. Furniture and belongings are carefully organized in order to make rooms look more spacious. For example, a living room can become a bedroom by adjusting the furniture at night.

(opposite page) Tokyo was once known as Edo, which means "gate of the river."

(below) A peaceful park just outside of the ancient city of Kyoto.

Japanese customs

Japanese culture is a balance of old customs and new ways of life. Match the pictures on these pages with the descriptions below to discover more about life in Japan.

Headbands

Headbands, or *hachimaki*, are worn to show that a person is preparing for a big mental, physical, or spiritual challenge. The *samurai* wore headbands under their helmets during battle. Today, Japanese people wear them for many important occasions such as festivals or during exam preparation.

Lantern lights

Long ago, Japanese people used paper lanterns to light their homes. Now these lights, painted with Japanese characters and symbols, are used for decoration. They are often used during festival celebrations.

Making use of rooftops

In Japan, where space is precious, rooftops serve as volleyball courts, public gardens, and even amusement parks. Department stores have pleasant rooftop gardens where shoppers can relax while their children play games.

Disneyland in Tokyo

The Sleeping Beauty Castle at Tokyo's Disneyland is a main attraction of this theme park. In every detail, this Disneyland is a **replica** of the original park in California. Japanese people are such passionate Mickey Mouse fans that they even have Mickey stores and Mickey hotels!

Model officers

Japan has an army of life-sized police officer models that stand by the side of the road or sit in patrol cars. These realistic models are meant to keep people from speeding along the highways. Recently, life-sized photographs of police have been added to this model brigade.

Glossary

ancestry The line of people from whom one is descended

artisan A craftsperson or skilled worker

cadmium A soft, bluish white metal that is mixed with other metals to create strong surfaces. It is dangerous to people's health.

ceremony A set of formal customs performed for a particular occasion

civilization A society with a well-established culture that has existed for a long period of time

clan A group of families that claims to have the same ancestors

climate The normal long-term weather conditions for an area

commuter train A train on which people travel long distances to work

culture The customs, beliefs, and arts of a distinct group of people

democracy A form of government in which people elect representatives to make decisions for society

descendants People who come from a particular family blood line

earth's crust The surface layer of the earth

electromagnet A magnet that is created by passing an electric current through a wire coil

erosion The gradual washing away of soil and rocks by rain, wind, or running water

feudal Relating to the class system of feudalism

feudalism A medieval class system based on the relationship between lords and the people who work for these lords

indigenous people The first people to live in a certain region or country

invader Someone who enters by force

kabuki A type of Japanese theatrical production

martial art A sport that uses warlike techniques for the purposes of self-defense and exercise

medieval Describing something that occurred during the Middle Ages (A.D. 500–1500)

mercury A silvery-white poisonous metal

miso Wheat, rice, or soybean paste to which water, salt, seaweed, and vegetables are added to make a soup

paddy A wet rice field

pagoda A tall, narrow building that looks like several one-story buildings stacked on top of one another

replica An exact copy of an original item

ritual A formal custom in which several steps are faithfully followed

sake A type of wine made from rice

tatami A standard-sized mat woven from rice straw

toxic Poisonous

trawling A way of fishing by dragging a strong net, shaped like a bag, along the ocean floor

tremor A shaking of the ground; an earthquake

Index

2 3 4 5 6 7 8 9 0   Printed in the USA   5 4 3 2